Looking at the Environment

David Suzuki

with BARBARA HEHNER

John Wiley & Sons, Inc.
New York • Chichester • Brisbane • Toronto • Singapore

Copyright © 1989, 1991 New Data Enterprises and Barbara Hehner

Published in Canada by Stoddart Publishing Co., Limited
First U.S. edition published by John Wiley & Sons, Inc., in 1992
Illustrations by Maureen Shaughnessy

This publication is designed to provide accurate and authoritative information in regard to the subject matter covered. It is sold with the understanding that the publisher is not engaged in rendering legal, accounting, or other professional service. If legal advice or other expert assistance is required, the services of a competent professional person should be sought. From a Declaration of Principles jointly adopted by a Committee of the American Bar Association and a Committee of Publishers.

Library of Congress Cataloging-in-Publication Data

Suzuki, David T.
    Looking at the environment / David Suzuki with Barbara Hehner
        p.   cm.
        Includes index.

        ISBN 0-471-54749-2 (lib. ed.)
        ISBN 0-471-54051-X (paper)

Printed in the United States of America

10 9 8 7 6 5 4 3 2 1

David Suzuki's Looking At Series

Looking at Weather
Looking at Senses
Looking at the Body
Looking at Insects
Looking at Plants
Looking at the Environment

Table of Contents

To Severn, Sarika and Joshua,
and to children everywhere who will inherit
what we adults make of the Earth
and
in memory of Chico Mendes

AN IMPORTANT NOTE FOR KIDS AND GROWNUPS
You will see this ✋ warning sign on some of the **Things to Do** in this book. It means that an adult should help out. The project may use some boiling water or something might need to be cut with a knife. Everyone needs to be extra careful. Most grownups will want to get involved in these projects anyway — why should kids have all the fun?

We're All In This Together

*E*nvironment is a word we hear a lot these days. Many TV programs and magazine articles talk about how the environment is being harmed by careless human beings. We make too much garbage and put poisonous chemicals in the air. But *what* exactly is the environment and *where* is it?

When you hop out of bed in the morning, you're in your environment. Your bed, your room, your whole house are part of your environment. The other people in your family are also part of your environment. In fact, *everything* around you, living and nonliving, makes up your environment. Your community is a larger environment that surrounds you.

Most of us live in cities or towns — in wood, brick, or concrete houses and apartment buildings. We buy most of our food and clothing in stores, ride in cars, and watch television. We human beings are smart enough to invent machines, and to plan and build the places we live in. It's often easy to forget that we are all still a part of *nature*.

Take a deep breath. You've just *inhaled* (breathed in) air into your lungs. Did you know that some of that air was once inside other people, and inside dogs, birds, trees, and houseflies? We inhale and *exhale* (breathe out) air that travels right around the world. This means we're sharing it with all the other air-breathing creatures on Earth.

Turn on the tap and take a drink of water. Did you know that some of the water was once part of the clouds in the sky? Some of it was inside forest trees; some was deep underground; and some was in rivers and streams. Water *recycles* endlessly.

Open your refrigerator or kitchen cupboard and look at the food. The meat, eggs, milk, bread, sugar, and fruit all came from plants and animals that were once alive. In fact, every single thing that we use for food was once living.

Now think about the objects in your home. The cotton sheets came from the seeds of a plant. The wool blanket was made from the hair of a sheep. Paper and wood came from parts of trees. The oil or gas for the furnace or car came from plants that lived millions of years ago. Without nature, we'd have no shelter, nothing to keep us warm, and nothing to eat. In fact, we wouldn't even be here!

As you can see, we depend on nature for the most important things in our lives. Even though we can build and invent many things, we still share the natural world with other animals and with plants. We even share it with tiny living things called *microorganisms* (they're so small that they can only be seen through a microscope). All of the living things on this Earth are connected together and we need each other. The rest of this book will explain why.

Share Your Environment

A few years ago, I had a visitor from another country staying with me. He really liked the bright, beautiful yellow flowers that he saw growing in fields and lawns. My visitor was surprised when I said that most Americans and Canadians try to get rid of their dandelions. When you can see certain flowers — or mountains, or snow, or beaches, or autumn trees — everywhere you look, you get used to them. You might still enjoy them, but you forget how amazing and beautiful they would look to someone who has never seen them before.

If you have friends or relatives who live far away from you, share your environment with them. If you live near the seashore, you can send them a pretty shell, or a small piece of driftwood. Or fill a small jar with fine white sand. If you live near some woods, you can send a fat pinecone. No matter where you live, you can usually find interesting stones, feathers, and pretty flowers that you can press. (Library books can tell you how to press and dry flowers.)

P.S. Maybe you don't have a faraway friend. Well, it isn't hard to make one. Get yourself a penpal. Children's magazines often have a penpal page. Many newspapers have a children's page that prints letters from kids looking for penpals. Penpals are a great way to find out about other parts of the world. You'll be amazed at all the different environments people call home.

How Has Your Environment Changed?

Can you remember the house or apartment you lived in five years ago? Was it bigger or smaller than your new one? Was it in the country? In a town? In a city? Even if you haven't moved in the last five years, your environment has very likely changed. Maybe your room has been repainted, or maybe an addition has been put on the house.

Look beyond your own home. Are there new buildings on your street? Do you think your neighborhood looks better or worse than it did five years ago? How much has your community changed in five years? It may look almost exactly the same, or it may look very different. Some quiet country towns near big cities have had many new houses and even apartment buildings built in them.

You could make a scrapbook or poster showing changes in your neighborhood. Maybe you could use some pictures from your family's photo collection (ask permission first). Or you could make drawings of how things were then and how they are now.

If you want to find out even more about how your environment has changed, here's what you can do. Talk to older people in your community about how things looked 40 or 50 years ago. Perhaps there were farmers' fields where city streets run now. Sometimes libraries have picture collections showing how your town or city looked 50 or even 100 years ago. Maybe they even have a picture of your street or house!

Night Creatures

Your backyard is part of your environment. You share it with all sorts of busy little creatures. There are some you usually don't see because they're *nocturnal*. That means they're active at night. Here's how to have a look at them without staying up all night.

What You Need:
a wide-mouthed glass jar
a garden trowel
a small, flat piece of wood
a few small stones or small
    wooden blocks

What to Do:

1. You're going to set up a trap for night creatures. It won't hurt them; it will just hold onto them until you get a look at them. You need to dig a hole in the ground for this. Ask permission *before* you dig.

2. Make a hole in the ground big enough to hold your jar. It should be deep enough that the mouth of the jar is level with the ground.

3. Cover the jar with a flat piece of wood. Use stones or blocks to hold it about half an inch (1 cm) above the jar. Your cover will keep the rain out. If rain got into your jar overnight, it could drown your captives.

4. Check your jar in the morning. What did you catch? You might find: ants, bugs, beetles, millipedes, centipedes, and other creatures. A library book about insects and other creepy-

crawlies will help you figure out who the night creatures are. Real insects have six legs. How many of your night creatures are insects?

5. Try digging your jar into the ground in other areas. You might get different insects under a tree than in the middle of a lawn. Do dry spots have more insects than wet spots?

After you've had a look at your creatures, let them go at the spot where you caught them.

A Long Way from Anywhere

Fewer than 300 people live on Tristan da Cunha in the South Atlantic Ocean. (Can you find this island on a globe or map?) If the islanders get tired of each other's company, they'd have a long way to go to find new friends. Their nearest neighbors are on the island of St. Helena, 1,320 miles (2,120 km) away!

The Living World

Suppose some smart and curious visitors came to Earth from outer space and looked around. They would quickly see that the world can be divided into two kinds of things: living and nonliving. The living world is made up of animals, plants, and microorganisms. The nonliving world is made up of rocks, air, water, and so on.

Most of the time, it's pretty easy to tell what's living and what's not. A stone is not living, while a rabbit and a tree are. But what about a piece of coral? If we look closely, we can see that one part of the coral is nonliving stuff as hard as rock. Inside its spaces, though, there are little animals. So we'd have to say that a coral reef is both living and nonliving.

How would our visitors from space tell the difference between life and nonlife? Being both smart and curious, they would use their special equipment to *magnify* the Earth's smallest organisms (make these tiny living things look bigger). Then they would look very carefully at how they were made. They would see that around each microorganism is a wall (which Earth scientists call a *membrane*). That membrane separates the inside of the organism from the outside world.

The membrane and everything inside it is called a *cell*. An organism can be made of just one cell or it can be made of many cells. An average grownup person, for instance, has 100,000,000,000,000 (that's a hundred *trillion*) cells! A cell can divide to make two identical cells. In fact, that's how you grow in size. As you grow up, your hands, feet, and other body parts get bigger because your cells are dividing.

A cell membrane, just like the wall of a house, has "doors" and "windows" to let things in and out. A cell grows and keeps itself healthy by taking in chemicals it needs through its membrane. Waste material can also be kicked out of the cell through the membrane. Cells can react to changes around them: movement up or down, heat or cold, darkness or light. They use food and try to get rid of poisons. Living things made of cells can do all these things. Nonliving things can't.

There are millions of different kinds of living things — plants and animals — on Earth. Each type of plant or animal that can *reproduce* (have offspring of the same kind) is called a *species*. How many species are there in the world? Scientists guess that there are between 10 and 30 million. Right now, they have found and named only about 1.4 million. But they know there are many left to discover, especially in the oceans and in tropical rainforests.

In the northern United States and in Canada, in about 2-1/2 acres (one hectare) of forest, we might find 10 to 20 different species of trees. In about 2-1/2 acres (one hectare) of rainforest along the Amazon River of South America, there might be 300 species of trees! One scientist found as many different species of ants on a single rainforest tree in Peru as there are in all of Great Britain. But people are now cutting down tropical rainforests so quickly that many species are becoming *extinct*. This means that they're disappearing forever from the Earth before scientists have even discovered them.

How many of the different groups of plants and animals are there? Of the 1.4 million species that scientists have found and named, 250,000 are plants. About 750,000 species are insects. About 41,000 species are *vertebrates* — animals with backbones. The rest of the species are microorganisms, fungi, and *invertebrates* — animals without backbones such as starfish, sponges, worms, and squid.

Of the vertebrates, about 25,000 species are fish, 9,000 are birds, 4,000 are reptiles, 3,500 are amphibians, and 4,300 are mammals. As you probably know already, we're one of the mammal species. We're in a group of 220 species called *primates*, along with gorillas and chimpanzees.

You can see that primates are greatly outnumbered by insects. In fact, over 90 percent of the world's animal species are insects. Before you run for a fly-swatter, though, consider this. Fewer than one in a thousand insect species cause trouble for human beings. Insects have an important place in the world. They help plants to grow, and they're food for thousands of animals. Besides that, when you look closely at a butterfly or a ladybug, you can see that insects are fascinating and often very beautiful.

AMAZING FACT

A Tiny Home for a Tiny Fish

The Devil's Hole pupfish lives in just one place in the world. This tiny fish swims around in a little pool on a certain rocky ledge in Nevada — and nowhere else in the world! During the summer, when the sun shines on the ledge, there may be 700 pupfish in the pool. In the winter, when there is no sunlight on the pool, the number of fish drops to about 200.

Amazing — and Endangered

In earlier books of the *Looking At* series, we talked about an amazing plant called the Rafflesia and an amazing insect called the Queen Alexandra Birdwing butterfly. Now both of them are on a list of endangered species put out by the IUCN. These letters stand for the International Union for the Conservation of Nature and Natural Resources. Its members are groups trying to protect the environment all over the world.

The Rafflesia of Sumatra is the world's largest flower. It's an orange-red giant that weighs about 26 pounds (12 kg). The Rafflesia lives on the roots of rainforest vines. As the rainforest is cut down, this rare, strange flower is disappearing. The Queen Alexandra Birdwing butterfly is found only in one part of Papua New Guinea. It is the world's largest butterly, with a wingspan of over 8 inches (21 cm). It can only live on one kind of vine, which twines 44 yards (40 m) up the trunks of tall trees. As farmers and loggers cut down the forests, the butterfly is losing its only home.

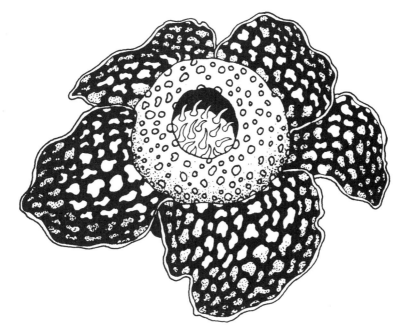

Go on a Track Hunt

The next time you go for an outdoor walk in a place where the ground is soft, look for animal footprints. If you take the right supplies along, you can even take some footprints home with you.

What You Need:
a knapsack or other carrying bag
a small sack of plaster of Paris
   (buy at a hardware or craft store)
a jar of water
an old stirring spoon
cardboard strips, about 5 inches (12
   cm) wide and 4 or 5 inches (10 to
   12 cm) long
a roll of tape
petroleum jelly (Vaseline)

What to Do:
1. Take a walk where the ground is soft but not soggy — along the bank of a stream, perhaps, or along a dirt path after a rainfall. Look for animal footprints.

2. When you find a good, clear footprint, carefully brush loose dirt, pebbles or grass away from it.

3. Tape a ring of cardboard to fit around the print. Push the ring of cardboard into the soil around the print.

4. Add plaster of Paris to the water, a little at a time, until the mixture looks like soft ice cream.

5. Pour the mixture over the footprint, to a depth of about 1 inch (3 cm). Let it harden. This will take about 20 minutes.

6. When the footprint mold is hard, lift it carefully and clean off loose dirt. Take it home with you.

7. Now you have a negative (raised) mold of the print you found. If you want to make a

positive print (sunk in like a footprint), you have more work to do at home.

8. Cover the negative print with petroleum jelly.

9. Make another ring of cardboard. It should be wide enough to stick up 1 inch (3 cm) above the negative print.

10. Pour plaster of Paris mixture over the negative print and let it set.

11. When the plaster of Paris has hardened, take the two molds apart. The second mold should be shaped just like the one you found on your walk.

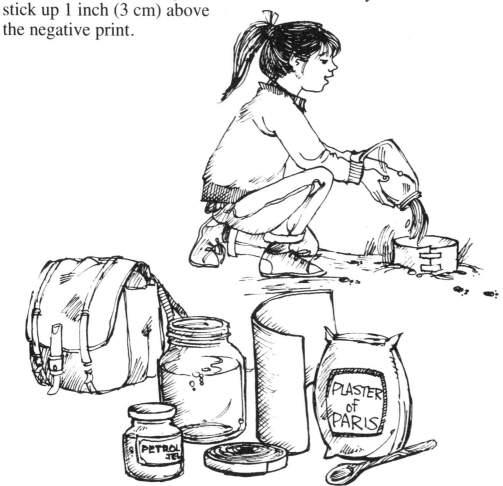

Worms at Work

Earthworms are called "the farmers' friends." As they tunnel through the ground, they make places where water and air can enter. Earthworms also turn over the soil, just as a person would with a hoe. They drag leaves and other bits of food down into the soil. As these things decay, they make the soil richer. Watch some worms at work.

What You Need:
a large wide-mouthed jar
some good, rich garden soil
some sand
worm food such as leafy vegetable
   bits, grass cuttings, carrot and
   potato peelings, coffee grounds
3 or 4 earthworms — the easiest
   time to find them is after a
   rainfall, when they come out of
   the ground
a piece from an old pair of sheer
   panty hose
an elastic band
a sheet of black construction paper

What to Do:
1. Fill the jar about 3/4 full with layers of sand and garden soil. Put in the layers this way: sand, soil, sand, soil. Moisten the layers so they're damp but not soaking wet. Too much water will kill the worms.

2. Put little bits of worm food on top. Place the worms in the jar.

3. Stretch the panty-hose piece over the top of the jar and hold it in place with the elastic band.

4. Worms don't like light. Tape black construction paper around the jar. Put the jar in a cool, dimly lit place. Every day, take away any food that is going bad and put fresh food bits on top of the soil. What kind of food do the worms like best?

5. Moisten the soil with a few drops of water if it needs it. Except for checking the food and water, try not to disturb the worms for about a week, so they can get used to their new home.

6. Now take a look at your worms. What changes have they made inside the jar? Are the sand and soil still in separate layers? Have the worms made tunnels? Can you see a worm dragging some food down from the top of the jar?

7. After you have taken care of your worms for a couple of weeks, let them go again where you found them.

What's Ecology?

Have you ever taken care of guppies or goldfish? If you have, you know how much work it takes to keep them healthy. You need to put a few water plants in their tank to keep the water fresh. These plants need sunlight, but not too much, or the water will overheat. You have to keep checking the water temperature. Maybe you add some snails to the tank to clean out the algae that grow there. Sometimes, though, the snails reproduce until there are too many for the tank. Then you have to take some out. You must keep adding water to the tank as it evaporates. And, of course, you have to feed the fish.

Do you ever wonder how these jobs are taken care of in a pond or a lake? Life goes on without a person around to drop in food, change the water, or add some plants and snails. Over millions and millions of years, plants, animals, and microorganisms have developed ways to stay in balance with each other.

Some biologists (scientists who study living things) specialize in *ecology*. The word ecology comes from Greek words meaning "the study of a household or home." In this case, "home" is the whole world of nature around us. Ecology looks at how living things live in their environment, taking things from it and giving things to it. An *ecosystem* is a community of creatures living together, all needing each other, and using nonliving things such as soil, water, and air. Ecosystems can be as small as a little pond or as big as a forest or desert.

Most plants and animals are suited to a certain *habitat* — just one special part of an ecosystem. For instance, a forest could provide many different habitats. Chipmunks burrow under tree roots. Gray squirrels make winter nests in tree trunks. Ruby-throated hummingbirds build dainty nests in leafy branches high above the ground. Even fallen, rotting trees can be homes. Raccoons and wolves may live in hollow logs. Sowbugs, centipedes, and millipedes scurry busily through damp rotting leaves on the forest floor.

When habitats are destroyed, most creatures who live there can't just move to a new location. Instead, they simply die out. So, when forests are completely cut down, what happens? When swamps are drained or filled in, when lakes and rivers are polluted or coral reefs are destroyed, what happens? Many of the creatures who lived there are homeless and may become *extinct*. This means that all the plants or animals of a species disappear from the Earth forever.

In an ecosystem, plants, animals, and microorganisms are in balance with each other. Even if that balance is upset for awhile, it has ways of coming

back. For instance, imagine a group of fieldmice who feed on certain plants. If the fieldmice have too many babies, they will eat so much that the plants they use for food will be used up. Then many of the mice will starve to death. However, as the number of mice falls, the plants will begin to grow back. In time, the mice and the plants will be back in balance.

The fieldmice also have an effect on other animals. Foxes eat fieldmice. If there are lots of fieldmice, the foxes will have more babies. On the other hand, if there are too many foxes and not enough mice to eat, some of the foxes will die. Then the number of mice will begin to go up again. And so it goes, around and around.

Sometimes, when a new species arrives somewhere, it will reproduce rapidly because there's nothing else to stop it. When Europeans settled in Australia, they brought in some animals from their home countries. Most of these animals couldn't live in Australia, so they died out. But rabbits lived there very well indeed. They had no enemies in Australia and multiplied quickly. Rabbits became pests who destroyed farm crops.

We human beings are a special species. We can live in many different environments. That's because we have used our brains to develop ways to survive. For instance, the Inuit in the Arctic know how to keep warm in extremely low temperatures. They know how to find food when it's completely dark day and night. They can build shelters in a blinding snowstorm. The !Kung people of Africa's Kalahari Desert can find water in the driest areas. (By the way, that exclamation mark stands for a special "clicking" sound in the !Kung language.) The !Kung can find food by following animal tracks or digging up edible roots. They can live under the searing hot sun of the desert.

Like every other human being, you've learned special skills for living in your environment. Can you think of some?

Go for a Sock Walk

Lots of plants need animals to spread their seeds. Some seeds are inside yummy fruit. Animals and birds eat the food. Then the seeds pass right through their digestive systems and end up on the ground again, somewhere else. Some seeds catch in animals' fur. They get spread around as the animals move from place to place. Put on some woolly socks and see how many seeds *you* can pick up.

What You Need:
a large pair of woolly socks, the
  fuzzier the better
a park or field to walk in
a summer or fall day, when weeds
  have ripe seeds
a magnifying glass

What to Do:
1. Pull the socks on *over* your
  shoes.

2. Go for a walk through the weeds
  in a field or park.

3. Take off the socks and see what
  seeds you've picked up. Are
  some seeds hard to pry off?
  Take a look at them through a
  magnifying glass to see what
  kind of "hooks" they have.

4. When you get home, you might
  like to try planting your seeds to
  see what kinds of plants come
  up. Egg cartons make good
  planters — you can put a
  different kind of seed in each
  place. Put your planter in a
  sunny spot and water it
  regularly. A library book about
  wild plants can help you figure
  out what you've got in your sock
  walk garden.

Garden under Glass

Create a small plant environment in a bottle.

What You Need:

a large clear glass bottle or jar with a lid (a wide-mouthed jar is easier to work with)

a few small green plants (you need plants that will grow slowly and stay small, such as maidenhair and bracken ferns, miniature ivy, and mosses)

small pebbles

some charcoal briquettes

a bag

a hammer

a strainer

potting soil

a piece of stiff paper

newspapers

What to Do:

1. Wash your bottle carefully with water and detergent. Rinse it very well and let it dry.

2. Spread out some newspapers to make a work surface.

3. Wash any dirt off your pebbles. Put pebbles in the bottom of your bottle. Your pebble layer should be about 1 inch (2-3 cm) deep.

4. Break up the charcoal into small pieces. Here is a tidy way to do it. Put the charcoal into a bag and break it up with a hammer. Ask a grownup to help you with this. Then pour the broken charcoal into a strainer and wash it under a tap.

5. Put one layer of charcoal into the bottle, on top of the pebbles. Your charcoal layer should be about 1/2 inch (1.5 cm) deep.

6. Make a funnel by rolling the piece of stiff paper. (See the drawing.) Put the funnel into the bottle and pour the potting soil through it. The funnel keeps the

sides of your bottle from getting dirty. You will need about 2 inches (5 cm) of soil.

7. Here's how to plan your garden. On a piece of paper, draw a circle the same size as your garden. Arrange the plants on the paper. When you are happy with the arrangement, plant them in the bottle. Don't crowd your garden. Remember that the plants will slowly grow and fill up the space.

8. Make holes in the soil for your plants. Gently lower the plants into the bottle and set them into their holes. Pat the soil down firmly around the base of each plant.

9. You might like to add small decorations to your bottle garden — maybe a shell or a little piece of driftwood.

10. Water the garden. It should be moist but not soaked. Put the lid

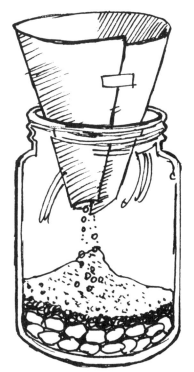

in place. As long as the lid is on, your garden will need only a little water every month or so.

11. Water your garden lightly, *only* if the soil seems dry. If the glass fogs up with water, your bottle garden has been watered too much. If this happens, take the lid off for a couple of days to let it dry out.

12. Put your bottle garden where it gets light, but don't set it in direct sunlight. Enjoy!

Moving Day Comes Twice a Year

Some animals need *two* habitats to meet their needs. Every year, they swim, fly, or walk from their winter homes to their summer homes. A few months later, they make the journey back. If only animals such as the gray whales could tell their stories to us. What epic adventures they must have on their long journeys! Gray whales migrate farther than any other mammals do. They make their way from the Bering Sea, where they spend the winter, south along the west coast of North America. This is a journey of 6,000 miles (9,650 km). The gray whales breed and have their calves in the waters off Baja, California. Then, in the fall, bringing their young ones, they make the long journey north again.

The Arctic tern is the mightiest migrator among birds. It travels 25,000 miles (40,200 km) — all the way from the North Pole to the South Pole — twice a year. Even some insects migrate. Monarch butterflies look too delicate to flutter more than a few yards (meters), but they make very long flights. These large black, white, and orange butterflies leave Canada in September and travel up to 1,850 miles (3,000 km) to reach their wintering grounds in Mexico, California, and Florida. Monarchs who make the journey south die before they can return. Their offspring, who have never seen Canada, somehow make their way north again in the spring.

Give and Take

Nature is full of examples of animals and plants who need each other to survive. When both living things are helped, the relationship is called *mutualism*. For instance, some kinds of little fish can swim unharmed into the jaws of bigger fish to pick their teeth. The little fish get a meal, and the bigger fish get their mouths cleaned of parasites. (And by the way, what's *parasitism*? That's a relationship in which one creature does all the taking and gives nothing back.)

Some of the most interesting pairs are made up of a plant and an animal. The slow-moving two-toed sloth spends its whole life in jungle greenery. Its fur is pretty greenish, too, thanks to algae that live in it. This special kind of algae can only grow on the coat of a sloth. So the algae get a good home, and the sloth gets a color that hides it from its enemies. Here's another example. Some ants live in the swollen thorns of acacia trees. The ants get food and safe shelter from the tree. But what, you ask, do the acacias get out of this? If any plant-eating animal so much as nudges the tree, the angry ants rush out and drive it away.

The Breath of Life

You can't see it, touch it, smell, it or taste it, but it's every bit as real as a mountain or a lake. Without it, you wouldn't be able to live. I'm talking about air. Try holding your breath for as long as you can. If you lasted for 60 seconds, you did very well. A person can live for weeks without food, and for a few days without water, but only for a couple of minutes without air. Without special air supplies, we can't go underwater or into space to explore.

But what is air? Air is a *gas*. This means that its molecules — the little particles that are the building blocks of all things — aren't packed together tightly enough to make a liquid or a solid. The two main ingredients of air are nitrogen and oxygen. Oxygen is the gas our lungs take out of the air when we breathe in. Air also has a little carbon dioxide (this is the gas plants "breathe in") and tiny amounts of some other gases. Finally, air contains water vapor (water in its gas form), and quite a bit of dust.

Although you can't see air, or grab a handful of it, you can tell that it's there. You can see the effects of air when trees bend in the wind. You can blow up a balloon and see the air make it big and round. You can feel air by blowing on your arm.

Air forms a protective wrapping around the Earth. We call this wrapping the *atmosphere*. The atmosphere keeps out a lot of the Sun's burning, harmful rays. It lets other rays go through, though, so that the Earth can be warmed. Where did this atmosphere come from?

Billions of years ago, when the Earth was new, its air was made up of gases that evaporated from its water, seeped out of its soil, and escaped from hot lava beneath the Earth's crust. This first atmosphere of Earth was a mixture of gases that today's land animals would not be able to breathe. When the first living organisms appeared in the oceans, there was still no oxygen in the air. Early plants changed the air by using up carbon dioxide and giving off oxygen. Over millions and millions of years, the air became the kind that we now breathe.

In the last hundred years, human beings have been causing the air to change once again. We've been cutting down vast areas of forest, which means there are fewer trees to take in carbon dioxide and give out oxygen. We've been releasing a lot of poisonous chemicals into the air from our cars and our factories. People used to say that air can't be seen or smelled. That's not true any more. In many cities today, we can see and smell the air because it's so dirty.

These changes in the air have given us lots of problems to worry about. Let's look at just one. You may have heard people talking about the "greenhouse effect." Perhaps you already know that it has something to do with the Earth getting warmer. But how does it happen and how can we stop it?

Have you ever noticed that, on a sunny day, a car gets extra hot inside? Rays of sunlight can come through the car's glass windows. But the heat they cause can't get back through the glass. Glass greenhouses use the same kind of trapped heat to help grow vegetables and flowers.

Some gases in the atmosphere, including carbon dioxide, can act just like that window glass. They let the Sun's rays through to warm the Earth. But they won't let the heat escape again. So the atmosphere could just get hotter and hotter. We know that the Earth is already almost 1.8°F (1°C) hotter than it was 200 years ago. That's when human beings started to put up factories, which add carbon dioxide and other gases to the atmosphere.

Higher temperatures could bring drought to the farmlands of many countries. Some people studying the greenhouse effect think that it could, after a long time, melt part of the polar ice cap. This would cause a huge rise in the level of the oceans. People studying the problem agree that the world has to cut down on the amount of carbon dioxide going into the air.

The Earth's air flows around the whole planet. When there's a dust storm over an African desert, some of the dust might blow all the way to North America. Chemicals sprayed on farmers' fields in Saskatchewan or Nebraska can be found at the North Pole. When a fire broke out at a nuclear power plant in Chernobyl in the Soviet Union, Sweden had radioactive chemicals in its air within a few hours. There's no way to keep air inside the borders of a country. All of us on Earth share the same atmosphere. And all countries have to work together to clean it up.

It's a Snap to Test for Polluted Air

Ozone and other gases in polluted air destroy rubber. Find out how good the air is where you live.

What You Need:
6 to 8 rubber bands (all the same size and thickness)
a coat hanger
a glass jar with a lid
a magnifying glass

What to Do:
1. Bend the coat hanger as shown in the drawing. You want it to hold the rubber bands straight without stretching them.

2. Slide 3 or 4 rubber bands onto the hanger. Hang the hanger outside in a *shady* place. (Sun also changes rubber, but you want to see what the air will do to the rubber bands without sunlight.)

3. Put 3 or 4 rubber bands into the glass jar. Close the lid tightly. Keep this jar indoors in a drawer or cupboard.

4. Wait a week. Check the rubber bands that have been outdoors. Use the magnifying glass to look at them more closely.

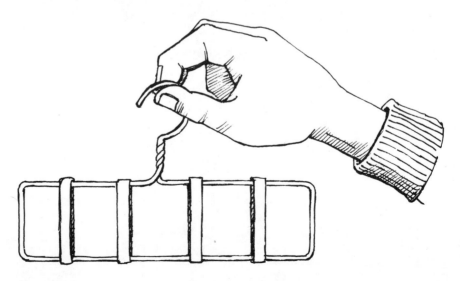

Do they have cracks or breaks?
Have any of them snapped?
How do they look compared with the rubber bands that were kept indoors in a jar?

5. If the outdoor rubber bands are still in good shape, put them back outside. Check them again in another week. Where the air is really polluted, rubber bands will snap in a week or two.

AMAZING FACT

The Case of the Disappearing Sunscreen

High in the atmosphere is a layer of gas called *ozone*. In 1977, a group of people studying this part of the atmosphere made a startling discovery. They found a hole in the ozone layer over the Antarctic. In the past 10 years this hole has become bigger. Now scientists have discovered another hole in the ozone. It's in the Arctic, over Baffin Island. Most people studying the ozone layer think it is being broken down by chemicals called CFCs. These chemicals are found in aerosol spray cans and refrigerator coolant. Why should we care if a gas in the upper atmosphere is disappearing?

Ozone shields the Earth from 90 percent of the Sun's ultraviolet (burning) rays. This is very important to us. If people receive too much ultraviolet radiation, they get a bad sunburn. Worse, after years of this, they may get skin cancer. Too much ultraviolet radiation will also kill food crops. In September 1987, 40 countries signed a treaty promising to cut the world's output of CFCs by 1994. But now many people feel that this is too little and want to get rid of CFCs much sooner. There's still time to save our ozone layer — and our skins.

Snare Dirt from the Air

Air may have tiny grains of sand, dust, ash, and other things floating in it. In Mexico City, which has a serious air-pollution problem, people have even found tiny bits of dung floating in the air. What kinds of solid stuff can you find in your air?

What You Need:
a white plate
petroleum jelly (Vaseline)
a magnifying glass

What to Do:
1. Cover the white plate with petroleum jelly.

2. Put the plate outside on a windowsill. Leave it there for a week.

3. Bring the plate in. Use the magnifying glass to see what has stuck to the plate. These are the solid bits and pieces that the air was carrying.

Our Watery Planet

On a hot day about 150 million years ago (give or take a few million!), a diplodocus lumbered to the edge of a pool. She bent down her long neck and drank thirstily. Maybe the glass of water you drank this morning was once inside that long-ago dinosaur. How could this be? For at least 3 billion years, Earth has been using the same water, over and over again.

Where do you think your glass of water came from? It could have come from a well underground, a lake, a reservoir, or a stream. But where did *that* water come from? It probably came from rain that fell from the clouds. But do you know where the rainwater comes from? It's not "new" water that arrives from somewhere in outer space. Rain is our own Earth water, coming back down to us again.

How does the water get up into the clouds, so that it can fall again as rain? It *evaporates* from lakes, seas, and other sources of water on Earth. When water evaporates, it seems to disappear, but it is not really gone. It has just changed from the liquid water we can see into a gas we can't see. *Water vapor* (water in gas form) rises from the Earth into the air. There it turns back into water, and falls as rain. This whole process is called the *water cycle*.

Earth is actually a very watery planet. Water and ice cover over 70 percent of the Earth's surface. Yet there are many places on Earth where people do not have enough water to wash with and to drink. How can this happen?

Well, 97 percent of the Earth's water is salty. People can't drink salt water. Another 2 percent of the Earth's water is frozen in glaciers and icebergs. Only about 1 percent is left where we can get it and use it — in lakes, rivers, and under the ground. Some parts of the world don't have lakes and rivers, and they have no way to pump up the deep groundwater.

Human beings, like other living things, need water to survive. In fact, our bodies are about 70 percent water. Every one of us needs about 2-1/2 quarts (2.4 L) of water every day, to replace what we lose by breathing, sweating, and going to the bathroom. We drink some of the water we need, and some of it comes from the food we eat.

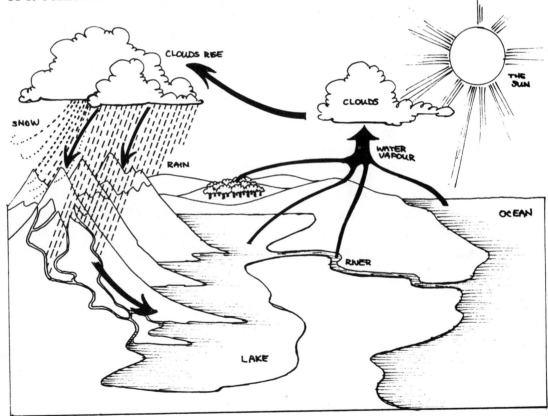

Of course, we use much more water than this. We wash ourselves, our clothes, our dishes, and so on. In fact, every person in North America uses about 58 gallons (265 L) of water every day. Some of this water is just plain wasted. We waste water by letting taps drip, by letting taps run hot or cold before using the water, and by washing tiny loads of laundry in great big washing machines. People in dry parts of the world have learned to make do with much less water than most North Americans use.

Earth's water resources are precious to us. Yet we're often careless with the water supply. For instance, people might spill oil or paint outside. These things can sink down through the ground until they reach the groundwater. If a big industry pours a lot of chemicals on the ground, or buries them, some of them will sink into the water below. Groundwater doesn't change much — it sits where it is for thousands of years. If we poison the water, the poison is there for thousands of years, too, and we have no way to clean it out.

Anything people do to change the water (and the air) in one place will change things for people far away. Acid rain is a problem like that. When industries' pollutants — especially sulfur dioxide and nitrogen oxide — rise into the air, they fall down from the sky again with the rain. Mixed with rainwater, they make acids — sulfuric acid and nitric acid. But most of the acid rain doesn't fall where it was made. Instead, winds blow it to other places, often hundreds of miles (kilometers) away.

When acid rain falls on the ground, it can take important plant foods out of the soil. This weakens trees so that many die. When acid falls into lakes, it can make them so acidic that water plants and fish are killed. Because the Earth's great water cycle cartwheels all around the world, problems like this can't be solved unless countries work together.

Cool, Clear Water

Most towns and cities get their water from lakes and rivers. This water has to be cleaned (purified) before it is safe to drink. Chemicals are added to the water to kill germs. The water flows through tanks with sand and gravel in them to filter out dirt. You can see for yourself how filtering works.

What You Need:
a pail full of muddy water
a clear plastic pop bottle
a paper coffee filter
some sand
some powdered charcoal

What to Do:

1. Ask an adult to cut the top of the bottle off for you, about 4 inches (10 cm) down from the mouth.

2. Turn the top of the bottle upside down. Set it in the bottom of the bottle, as shown in the drawing.

3. Put a coffee filter in the upside-down section. Put a layer of sand in the filter. On top of the

sand, put a layer of charcoal. Then add another layer of sand.

4. Slowly pour the muddy water into the filter. Don't let it overflow. The water will drip through the sand and charcoal into the bottle underneath. How does the water look now?

WARNING: Although the water now looks much cleaner, *it is not safe to drink.* In a real water purification plant, chemicals are added to kill germs in the water.

What's Happening?

Water purification plants take lake or river water and make it flow through a series of tanks. Chemicals are added to take away bad tastes and smells and to kill germs. As the water goes from tank to tank, the solid bits of dirt sink to the bottom. Finally the water is filtered through sand and gravel to catch other, smaller bits of dirt. The clean water goes into a holding tank, ready to be piped to your house.

AMAZING FACT

Danger: Acid Shock!

What's the most dangerous season for many North American lakes? Springtime! Snowfalls, just like rainfalls, can be full of acid from air pollution. All winter long, the snow piles up on the ground. The acid trapped in the snow builds up, too. When the snow melts in the spring, all this acid is suddenly released. A lot of it pours into lakes. Sometimes the acid level in a lake can become 1,000 times greater in just a couple of weeks. This sudden "acid shock" kills insects, frogs, and even fish such as trout and salmon.

Hatch Some Brine Shrimp

You won't find brine shrimp in your local pond, or even at the seashore. They can live only in *very* salty water, such as the Great Salt Lake in Utah, U.S.A. But pet stores sell brine shrimp eggs as fish food. Here's how to hatch them.

What You Need:

dried brine shrimp eggs from a pet store (Shrimp eggs won't hatch unless they are dried out first.)

a large, wide-mouthed jar, carefully washed

6 tablespoons (90 mL) *non-iodized* salt (Pickling salt is usually non-iodized. If iodine has been added to the salt, it will say *iodized* on the box—this is poison for the shrimps.)

1 tablespoon (15 mL) Epsom salts

1/2 teaspoon (2 mL) borax

packages of active dry yeast

a wax crayon

a magnifying glass

a large measuring cup

water

What to Do:

1. Fill the jar with tap water. Let the jar stand *for at least a day* to get rid of the chlorine in it. Make a crayon mark on the jar to show the water level.

2. Add the salt, Epsom salts, and borax to the water. Stir the water until all the salts are dissolved. (When they're dissolved, you can't see them anymore.)

3. Add a pinch of brine shrimp eggs — about 50 tiny eggs — to the water.

4. Place the jar in a warm, sunny indoor spot. (The best hatching

temperatures are 75°F to 90°F (24°C to 32°C). The shrimp will hatch in about a day.

5. When all the eggs are hatched, pour about 1/2 cup (120 mL) of water into a large measuring cup. Add one package (about 1 tablespoon, or 15 mL) of yeast to the water to make a milky mixture. It will foam up as it stands, but that's OK.

6. Add a little yeast and water to the jar, until the jar water is *just a bit* cloudy. As the shrimp eat the yeast, the water will turn clear again. Add a little yeast-water every day.

7. If you look at the hatched eggs through a magnifying glass, this is what you will see: The young shrimp break out of the eggshell, but they are still in transparent ("see-through") sacs. After about a day, the young shrimp swim out of their sacs. Each one has an eye spot, and three pairs of antennae. Later, each shrimp will develop many pairs of legs.

8. Keep the jar in sunlight. Green algae will begin to grow in the water, and the shrimp will eat this too.

YOUNG BRINE SHRIMP

ADULT BRINE SHRIMP

NEWLY HATCHED, STILL IN SAC

EGG

EPSOM SALTS

SEA SALT

BRINE SHRIMP EGGS DRIED

YEAST

BORAX

9. As water evaporates from the jar, the water level will go down. Add a little tap water (*not* salt water) to bring the water up to the crayon mark you made.

10. The trickiest thing about raising brine shrimp is to give them the right amount of food. Too much yeast will poison the water and kill the shrimp. If this happens, try again with fresh water and another small batch of eggs.

11. If you are able to keep your brine shrimp alive for 3 weeks or so, they will become adult shrimp about 1/4 inch (6 mm) long. If you look at them through a magnifying glass, you will see their many pairs of paddling legs.

AMAZING FACT

Acid Rain Makes Sour Notes

What does acid rain have to do with off-key church bells? In the Netherlands, the answer is: a lot. This country has about 15,000 bells in its many bell towers. In recent years, the bells just haven't sounded the way they should. *Carilloneurs* (people who give concerts by playing sets of bells) find that their bells aren't in tune anymore. The cause is acid rain, which has eaten into the metal bells. As the bells become thinner, they sound lower notes than before. Worse, smaller bells are eaten away more quickly than bigger bells. This means that *carillons* (sets of bells) don't stay in tune with each other. For now, the Dutch are scraping metal off the big bells until they're as thin as the small ones. In the long run, though, the bells will go out of tune again — unless acid rain stops falling on them.

You Are What You Eat

What did you have for dinner last night? Pork chops? Couscous? Lasagna? It would be hard for me to guess, because people can eat so many different things. Still, I know you didn't go out to a field and graze on grass. And I know you didn't go for a swim so that you could scoop up tiny water plants in your mouth.

All animals — including human beings — have to eat. Food is the fuel that gives their bodies the energy they need to live. But different kinds of animals need different kinds of fuel. Their bodies will only *digest* (break down and use) some things. Other things just pass right through their digestive systems or even make them sick.

Carnivores (from the Latin word for "flesh-eaters") are animals that eat meat. Sharks, lions, and eagles are carnivores — and so is a house cat. You might wish that your cat would not kill mice and birds. But you can't just feed him stringbeans instead. His body needs meat. Carnivores that kill animals and eat them are called *predators*. The animals they eat are called *prey*.

Some carnivores eat animals that are already dead. They're called *scavengers*. Crows, vultures, and hyenas are scavengers. Have you ever seen crows sitting by the roadside, pecking at the body of a dead animal? Sometimes the sight makes us shudder. Without scavengers, though, the Earth would pile up with animal carcasses.

Herbivores, as you can probably guess, are the plant-eating animals. Mice, cows, and chickadees are herbivores. Some animals eat both meat and plants. They're called *omnivores* ("everything-eaters"). Raccoons and bears are omnivores. What are you — a carnivore, a herbivore, or an omnivore?

Animals and plants, you remember, live together in communities called ecosystems. All the living things in an ecosystem are linked together in *food chains*. Here's an example of a food chain:

This is the grass.

This is the grasshopper that eats the grass.

This is the frog that eats the grasshopper that eats the grass.

This is the snake that eats the frog that eats the grasshopper that eats the grass.

At the bottom of this food chain is a plant. At the top of the chain is a "third-order carnivore" — something (snake) that eats something (frog) that eats something (grasshopper) that eats a plant. Can you think of some food chains that have you somewhere in them? Are human beings always at the top of a food chain?

Food chains always start with plants. That's because plants are the only living things that can capture the Sun's energy and use it to make their own food. A plant's way of making food is called *photosynthesis*. Photosynthesis comes from two Greek words. *Photo* means light and *synthesis* means putting things together in a new way. Green plants have a special chemical in their leaves called *chlorophyll*. Chlorophyll lets plants use energy from sunlight to make food out of carbon dioxide and water. Plants take carbon dioxide out of the air. They usually take the water they need out of the soil.

In a way, plants are the only food on Earth. To get energy, all animals must either eat plants, or eat animals that eat plants. The higher up the food chain an animal is, the more plants are needed to feed the animal. A field of clover could be enough food for 100 mice — but the mice might only be enough food for two owls. Why is this so? At each "link" of the food chain, some energy is lost from the chain. For instance, suppose a mouse eats a few sprigs of clover. The mouse gets some of the clover's stored energy. But the mouse also uses up energy, breathing and running around. When an owl eats the mouse, the owl gets some of the energy the mouse took from the clover, but not all of it.

Because energy is always being lost from food chains, new energy from the Sun is always needed. And the Earth needs lots of plants to turn the Sun's energy into food for us and other animals.

Food Chain Mobiles

Explore some food chains — and turn them into colorful art!

What You Need:
twigs and small branches of different lengths (find ones that have
    fallen on the ground)
string, strong thread, or wool
old nature magazines or calendars you can cut up, or art supplies
    to make your own pictures

What to Do:
1. Read some library books about animals to find out about food chains. Ask the librarian for help in finding the right books.

    Here's one way to work out a food chain. Start with a carnivore that interests you — maybe an owl or a lion. Read about it and find out what it eats. The owl, for instance, eats mice. Then read about mice and find out what *they* eat. Now you've got a food chain with three things in it. How long a food chain can you find? Can you work out a food chain with *you* in it?

2. Find or draw pictures of the living things in your food chains. To make a mobile, you need at least three food chains with at least three things in each one. Look at the drawing on the facing page to see how to arrange your mobile.

3. Tape a short piece of thread, string, or wool to the top of each picture. Make sure the picture hangs straight.

4. Now tie the string holding the first picture in a food chain to one end of a twig or branch. Tie the string of the last picture to

the other end. Space the other pictures in between. Make two more food-chain branches like this.

5. Find your longest branch. It should be long enough so that 3 smaller branches can hang from it. (Look at the drawing on this page.)

6. Take two squares of paper. Print FOOD on one, and CHAINS on the other. Tape string to them and hang them from a small branch.

7. Join all the branches together with string, as shown in the drawing. Always tie the string to the middle of each branch, so that the branch hangs straight.

8. Hang up your mobile and enjoy it.

Banquets for Birds

It's easy to feed the birds. You can just scatter food for them on the ground or on a windowsill. Or you can make simple birdfeeders out of old containers. That way, you can do some recycling at the same time.

1. Windowsill Bird Feeding

Jays, nuthatches, and cardinals are bold, curious birds. They will fly right onto a window ledge for a meal. Start by putting bread crumbs on a windowsill. Birds can spot them quickly. When the birds are used to coming to your house to eat, you can switch to sunflower seeds or wild birdseed.

Here's a quick windowsill treat: Roll 1 cup (250 mL) of peanut butter in birdseed or sunflower seeds to make a ball. Squeeze it in your hands until it holds together well. Put the ball on your windowsill. (If you have a backyard, you can also put it out on a fencepost.)

2. Scattered Food

The easiest way to feed backyard birds is to scatter breadcrumbs or seed on an open patch of ground. Another treat some birds like is crushed dog biscuits. Put several biscuits in a bag and close it tightly with a twist tie. Break up the biscuits with a rolling pin until they're fine crumbs. Scatter them outside.

If you have a fireplace, here's something else you can do to help the birds in winter. Put cold ashes from the fireplace near the bird food. Or crush eggshells into fine grit and put them out. Birds need to swallow bits of grit to help them digest their food. Once the ground is covered in snow, it's hard for them to find this grit.

3. Doughnut Feeder

2 plastic or metal jar lids
a long nail
a long bolt with a nut
a hammer
a doughnut
a length of string

1. Ask permission before using the hammer. Work at a workbench, or on top of a piece of scrap wood. Otherwise, you could damage a table or floor with your hammering.

2. Hammer the nail through the center of each lid. Twist the nail around to make the holes a little bigger.

3. Push the bolt through one lid. Then slide the doughnut onto the bolt. Put the second lid on the bolt and push it up against the doughnut. Screw on the nut to hold the lid in place.

4. Use the string to hang the doughnut feeder from a tree branch.

4. Milk Carton Feeder

an empty milk carton, 1/2 gallon (2 L) size, well washed
scissors
a plastic straw or thin wooden dowel
a ruler
a nail for punching holes

1. Cut one side of the carton off, stopping 1-1/2 inches (4 cm) from the bottom, as shown in drawing 1.

2. Measure 1-1/2 inches (4 cm) in from the cut side edges, as shown in drawing 2. Cut off these extra pieces. Now you have a place for a bird perch, and an overhanging roof to keep visiting birds dry.

3. Punch two holes and put the plastic straw or dowel across the bottom to make a perch. Punch another hole in the top and hang the feeder from a tree. Or you can nail the back of the feeder to a post.

4. Put birdseed in the feeder and see who comes to dine.

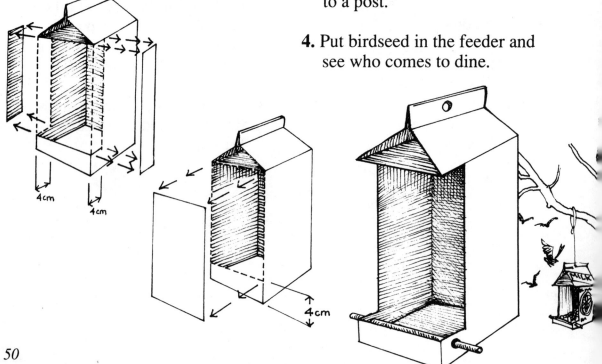

5. Margarine Tub Feeder

2 empty plastic margarine tubs,
   one about 1 pound (500 g) size,
   and one about 1/2 pound (250 g)
   size
a plastic straw
nylon string
a nail to poke holes

1. Use the nail to poke a hole in the middle of the bottom of each margarine container. Poke a hole in the middle of the big container's lid.

2. Thread the nylon string through all the pieces as shown in the drawing. The big container, turned upside down, makes the roof. The straw, threaded on the string, helps to hold up the roof. The small container is the dish of food. The lid of the big container is a tray at the bottom.

3. When all parts are threaded, tie a knot in the string to keep them all together. Then tie the string to a tree branch and fill the dish with birdseed.

Bird Feeding Tips:

If you can, set up two or three bird-feeding stations. Some birds are bullies. Once they find an eating spot, they will drive other birds away. If there are several eating places, all the birds have a better chance to get their share.

Once you start feeding the birds, *don't stop*. They will come to depend on you for food. If you stop suddenly in the winter, they may starve.

Who Likes What:

Sunflower Seeds: Jays, cardinals, chickadees, goldfinches, nuthatches, sparrows.

Millet: Juncos, sparrows, goldfinches, snow buntings, redpolls.

Peanuts: Jays, chickadees, goldfinches.

Suet and Bacon Fat: Woodpeckers, chickadees, starlings.*

* To learn how to make an easy suet feeder, see p. 54.

Squirrel Obstacle Course

In many parts of North America, it's hard to
feed the birds without feeding gray squirrels too.
People have tried greased poles and tippy plates under
the feeder. These are supposed to make squirrels slip off. Often the clever
squirrels get to the food anyway. Some people in Britain who were making a
film about gray squirrels decided to give them a test. They made a squirrel
obstacle course, with a feeder full of peanuts at one end.

To get to the food, the squirrels had to climb a pole, scamper across a rope, run
through a tunnel, and jump to a seesaw. As they walked along the seesaw, it
tipped, and the squirrels had to jump to another platform. Then the squirrels had
to go along a length of chain, through another tunnel, and walk along another
rope. (Most squirrels crossed the rope paw over paw, hanging upside down.)
Finally, the squirrels had to go up a chimney and take a flying leap to the last
pole and the peanut tray. The whole course was almost 45 feet (14 m) long.
The first squirrel who finished the course took 2 weeks and 2 days to figure
it out. Soon all the squirrels in the group could do it. After a few practice
runs, they could reach the peanuts in just 24 seconds!

Suet Suits Birds Just Fine

Chickadees, starlings, nuthatches, and other birds can get a burst of energy from these suet cupcakes.

What You Need:

Cupcake ingredients:

1/2 cup (125 mL) beef suet (hard beef fat — ask for it if you don't see it at the grocery store meat counter)
1/2 cup (125 mL) peanut butter
3 cups (750 mL) cornmeal
a muffin tin with 12 cups
paper cupcake cups
a kitchen knife
a stirring spoon
a double boiler
oven mitts
a mesh bag, such as the kind onions are sold in

What to Do:

1. Line the muffin cups with the paper cupcake cups.

2. Get permission from an adult before you use the stove. Put some water in the bottom of the double boiler. Heat it until it is just starting to roll and bubble. Turn the heat to low.

3. Cut the suet into small pieces. If you're not allowed to use kitchen knives, ask an adult to help you with this part. Put the suet pieces in the top of the double boiler on the stove, and stir them until they melt.

4. Stir in the peanut butter and the cornmeal.

5. Put on oven mitts. Carefully pour the hot mixture into the muffin cups. Let the muffins sit until they're cool and firm.

6. Peel off the papers. Put 3 or 4 muffins in the mesh bag. Hang the bag from a tree branch.

(Store the other muffins in the freezer. You can use them to feed the birds another time.)

AMAZING FACT

The World's Biggest Appetite?

Deep, deep in the ocean lives a strange fish. It's known as the *giant swallower*, not because it is a big fish, but because it can eat such enormous meals. The swallower is less than 4 inches (10 cm) long. However, a research ship recently hauled up a swallower that looked hugely swollen. An x-ray of the fish showed it had swallowed an eel 15 inches (38 cm) long. The eel was curled round and round in the fish's stomach.

A fish this full of dinner can hardly move. So why would it eat so much? People who study deep-sea fish think they might know the answer. Where the swallower lives, 6,000 feet (1,800 m) down in the ocean, there is no sunlight at all. There are no plants, and no plant-eaters. The few fish here are meat-eaters, preying on each other. A meal doesn't swim past very often, so the swallower probably has to grab food when it can. Wouldn't you?

BEFORE DINNER

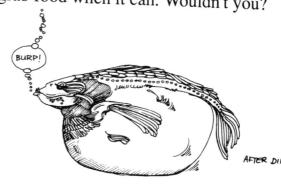

BURP!

AFTER DINNER

Try a Vegetarian Meal

A huge amount of grain is needed to feed cattle and other animals so that we can eat them later. If people ate the grain — or other plants — instead, more people could be fed at lower cost. Try a vegetarian meal, and move yourself down the food chain.

What You Need:
a large cooking pot
a seive or colander
a frypan
stirring spoons
a knife for cutting vegetables
a cheese grater
measuring spoons
a large serving bowl

Ingredients for Macaroni Salad:*

8 ounces (225 g) macaroni
6 tablespoons (90 mL) olive or
    sesame oil
4 ounces (100 g) blanched almonds
4 ounces (100 g) canned, sliced
    mushrooms
1/2 small onion, diced
2 sticks celery, chopped
4 ounces (100 g) grated cheese
juice of 1 lemon

a pinch of cayenne pepper (this
    means pinch a few grains
    between your fingers)
2 eggs, hardboiled, shelled, and
    sliced
1 ounce (25 g) roasted sunflower
    seeds
salt

What to Do:
1. Bring a large pot of salted water to a boil. Add the macaroni and cook it according to the package directions.

2. While the macaroni is cooking, chop the onion and celery. Ask permission to use the knife. If you're not allowed to use kitchen knives yet, ask an older person to do this part. Grate the cheese.

3. Drain the macaroni through the sieve or colander into the sink. This is tricky, because the pot will be heavy and the water will be very hot. Ask an adult to do this.

4. Run cold water over the macaroni and drain it again. Put the cooked macaroni into the large serving bowl. Add 1 tablespoon (15 mL) of oil and stir it into the macaroni.

5. Put 1 tablespoon (15 mL) of oil in the frypan. Over medium heat, fry the almonds in the pan until they are just browned. Stir them and keep an eye on them all the time. Then add the mushrooms and fry them, stirring, for 1 or 2 minutes.

6. Add the things in the frypan to the bowl of macaroni. Add the remaining 4 tablespoons (60 mL) of oil to the bowl. Then add all the other ingredients. Add just a little

sprinkle of salt. Taste the salad to see if it's salted enough, before you add any more. Mix all the ingredients together well. Enjoy your salad.

If you want an even more nutritious meal, serve your macaroni salad with a salad of lettuce, small cubes of cheese, olives, and tomatoes.

* This is a lacto-vegetarian meal. Even though lacto-vegetarians don't eat meat, they do eat eggs, milk, cheese, and other dairy products.

What A Waste!

Have you ever had a pet cat, dog or budgie? What do you do to take care of a pet? You have to feed it, of course. You also have to clean up after it. A cat has a litter box. A dog may have a special corner of the backyard. Budgie droppings fall on the paper in the bottom of the bird's cage. You may think it would be nice to have a pet that never had to go to the bathroom. That's impossible, though. All living organisms must have water and food and they all produce *wastes*. If they didn't get rid of their body wastes, these wastes would poison them.

What's amazing is that the wastes of one organism can be useful for another organism. For instance, we breathe out a gas called carbon dioxide. It's a waste from our lungs. But plants need carbon dioxide to live. Plants "breathe out" oxygen through their leaves because they don't need it. We breathe in oxygen to stay alive.

Every year, autumn leaves fall from the trees. Maybe it's your job to rake them up. Have you ever wondered what happens to leaves that fall in the woods? Nobody rakes them up, but the leaves don't pile up higher and higher. That's because they *decay*. Bacteria and molds grow on the leaves, breaking them down into smaller bits. These bits are food for worms, insects, and plants.

After a rabbit dies in the woods, a crow may come along and eat it. Flies may lay eggs on it and other insects may carry off bits of it. Finally bacteria will break the body down. All the useful chemicals that were inside the dead animal will end up inside living animals, or back in the ground where plants can use them.

The valuable things on our planet aren't endless. There is only so much air, water, and soil, and every living thing has to share them. Nature keeps recycling things, using them over and over again. Unfortunately, people aren't always so good at dealing with wastes.

Most human beings live in large groups, in cities and towns. That means we have a special problem of getting rid of all the wastes that we produce in one place. Moreover, we human beings are very different from other creatures because we make things out of stone, bricks, glass, clay, and metals. These things don't recycle naturally like *organic* things — things that were once alive. We human beings also create new materials such as plastics and chemicals that never existed on Earth before. Usually there's nothing in nature that uses these things by breaking them down. That's why a lot of garbage produced by human beings builds up in the environment.

In the past, people didn't throw much away. They saved string and paper bags to use again. They took old clothes apart. The least-worn parts were resewn into children's clothes or bed covers. Finally the almost wornout

cloth was used as cleaning rags. Nearly everybody recycled as much as they could. In poorer countries today, many people still use things over and over.

In the past 20 years or so, however, we in the world's richer countries have begun to use many disposable (throwaway) things. Today many cities and towns are running out of places to dump their garbage. Many of the chemicals in our wastes slowly leak into the ground, the water, and the air, polluting the environment.

In North America, the average person at home produces over 2 pounds (1 kg) of garbage every day. If we add in the waste produced by people at work, it comes to over 4 pounds (2 kg) a day. What's in this garbage? About 37 percent of it is paper; about 10 percent of it is glass; and almost 10 percent of it is metals. About 9 percent is plastics, just over 8 percent is food, and just under 18 percent is yard wastes. Most food and yard wastes could be composted. (*See page 61.*) Although most of the other things cannot be recycled in nature, people now know how to break them down and use them again. We know how to reuse paper, glass, and metals, and we are working on the problem of melting down and reusing plastic.

Recycling makes sense. For instance, it takes a lot of work to dig metal out of the ground and process it to make aluminum cans. If we just melt down aluminum cans and use the metal over again, it takes only 10 percent of the energy it took to make the original can. In most cities and towns today, people can recycle old newspapers, glass jars, and metal cans. Recycling saves money and energy and cuts down on pollution. Recycling helps save the environment, so that you will still be able to enjoy clean air and pure water when you're grown up. How much are you recycling at your house?

Garbage In, Compost Out

Can you really make something useful out of raked-up leaves and vegetable peelings? Yes, you can make a great soil conditioner for your garden.

What You Need:
a big plastic garbage can with a lid
   (the outdoor kind)
a long stick to stir the compost
soil
compost ingredients, described
   below

What to Do:
1. Ask an adult to poke 20 to 30 small holes in the lid, sides, and bottom of the garbage can. The holes are to let air in. The ones in the bottom are needed to allow extra water to drain out.

2. Put some garden soil in the bottom of the garbage can. Now add some fruit and vegetable garbage — peelings, skins, coffee grounds, carrot tops, and any other leftovers that were about to be thrown out. Don't put any meat or bones in your compost, as these can attract flies and rats. When you are starting your compost, put about as much vegetable garbage in the can as you put soil.

3. Add some decaying leaves and grass clippings.

4. Add some soil-stirring animals, such as earthworms and sow bugs.

5. Stir the compost with the stick. Compost should be damp but not soaking wet. Sprinkle a little water on if it is too dry. Add dry soil if the compost mix is too wet.

6. Add more vegetable garbage every time you have some. Each time, add a little soil to go with it. Stir the mixture every 2 or 3 days.

7. When the can is about 3/4 full, stop adding garbage and let it sit for 3 to 6 weeks. By that time, you should have crumbly, rich compost for your garden. If it's still a bit lumpy, you can strain it through an old window screen when you put it on the garden.

SOMETHING TO DO

Plant a Garbage Garden

Some things are *biodegradable*. This means that bacteria and other microorganisms in the soil can break them down. Other things cannot be broken down. Find out which things are which.

What You Need:
as "plants" for your garden, choose some things from this list:

a piece of pure cotton cloth (perhaps from an old tea towel or T-shirt)
different kinds of paper — a square of toilet paper, a piece of writing paper, a piece of newspaper, a piece of shiny magazine paper
a styrofoam cup or hamburger box
a piece of aluminum foil
an apple or pear core
a plastic sandwich bag or piece of plastic wrap
a piece of wool cloth (perhaps part of a wool mitten that has lost its mate)
a garden trowel
a watering can or hose
popsicle sticks
an area of soil, perhaps in your backyard or in a large plant pot or box

What to Do:

1. Ask permission *before* you dig holes for your garbage garden. Dig holes about 4 inches (10 cm) deep. Dig one hole for each thing you're planting.

2. Put a little water into each hole. Put a garbage "plant" in each hole. Cover with earth. Put a popsicle stick at each spot so you'll know where the things are.

3. Water your garden every day for about a month. Then dig the things up again. How do they look? Which things are starting to break down? Which things look just as they did when you planted them? (Being wet and dirty doesn't count as a change!)

63

How Degrading!

Some brands of toilet paper are more biodegradable than others. Find out how fast some different brands break up in water.

What You Need:

squares of as many different brands of toilet paper as you can get. Ask friends and relatives for squares from their houses, and get some pieces of the kinds used in restaurant and school washrooms, too.

wide-mouthed jars with lids — one jar for each kind of toilet paper. All the jars should be the same size.

sticky tape

What to Do:

1. Cut or tear two small pieces from each kind of toilet paper. Keep all your pieces the same size.

2. Tape one piece on the outside of the jar so you know what kind you put inside. You can write the brand name — if you know it — on the outside piece. Put the other piece inside the jar.

3. Do the same thing with every kind of toilet paper you have. Fill the jars with water and put their lids on tightly.

4. Shake each jar 20 times. Have any of the papers started to change?

5. Leave the jars for a week. Then shake them again in the same way. Which kind of toilet paper has broken down the most? Which kind has broken down the least? Do you notice a difference between colored and white paper in speed of breaking down? Which kind of toilet paper do you think would pollute the environment the most? The least?

More to Think About:

Why do you think it was important for all the paper pieces and all the jars to be the same size? Why did you need to shake all the jars the same number of times?

AMAZING FACT

Something's Under the Bed!

Yes, something really is under your bed right now — and in your carpet and even *in* your bed. Chomp, chomp, chomp! Millions of tiny, busy dust mites live in house dust. They're dining on their favorite food — little flakes of your skin.

The outer layer of your skin is flaking off all the time. (Don't worry. It's being replaced, so you don't miss it!) In fact, skin flakes are a big part of house dust. Dust mites help clean it up. They're too small to see. Three dust mites would fit on the period at the end of this sentence. They don't cause problems for most of us. Some people, though, wheeze and sneeze in dusty rooms. What's bothering them is not the dust, but the droppings of the dust mites who live in it.

Bottle Music

Good for you — you've saved up lots of bottles for recycling. Have some fun with them before you turn them in.

What You Need:
8 glass pop bottles, all the same size and shape
water
a stick to tap the bottles

What to Do:

1. Fill the first bottle with water, almost to the top. This is your scale's lowest note — "Do" or C. Tap the bottle with the stick and listen to the note.

2. Fill the second bottle with about 1 inch (2 cm) less water than the first one. This bottle will be "Re" or D. If the note isn't right, add or take away water. (You can tune your bottles to a piano or other musical instrument if you have one.)

3. Fill the rest of the bottles with water. Each bottle should have a little less water than the one before it. "Tune" them by adding or taking away water, so you can play the scale, "Do, Re, Mi, Fa, Sol, La, Ti, Do" on them.

Tuning a bottle orchestra can be tricky. Sometimes the bottles don't have the same thickness of glass, so two bottles with the same amount of water give different notes. If all this tinkering is getting you nowhere, ask an older person to help you. Try to find one who has some musical training.

4. Now try out some simple tunes
on your bottles. Here's one to
get you started:

EDCD EEE DDD EGG EDCD EEE EDDEDC
or
Mi Re Do Re   Mi Mi Mi   Re Re Re   Mi Sol Sol
Mi Re Do Re   Mi Mi Mi   Mi Re Re Mi Re Do

Do you know the song? What else can you play?
P.S. Don't forget to recycle the bottles!

AMAZING FACT

Le Stink!

When tourists plan to go to Paris, France, they usually look forward to seeing the Eiffel Tower. However, another big tourist attraction in Paris is under the city — the sewer system! Every Monday and Wednesday afternoon, guides lead people through dripping tunnels, past smelly waste-collection pits. A dirty gray river of sewer water flows past them. People also visit a museum of sewer history with an audio-visual display.

The sewer tunnels make a vast, mysterious underground city. Laid end to end, they could stretch over 1,200 miles (2,000 km). Of course, tourists only visit a small part of them — as long as they don't get lost on the tour!

Wooden Giants

They are living things much bigger than we are. They can live much longer than we do — sometimes hundreds or even thousands of years. They stand all around us, but they never say anything. Don't worry, I'm not talking about aliens, I'm talking about trees! Trees are the oldest living things on Earth. There are trees alive today that were growing when the pyramids were built in ancient Egypt. If trees could talk, think of the stories they could tell.

In cities, we see trees growing here and there on streets and in yards and parks. But only a few hundred years ago, much of North America was one huge forest. Once, all of Europe and a lot of Africa, India, and China were also covered with thick forests. Today, only about 30 percent of the world is forested. That amount is dropping very quickly. Every *minute*, an area of tropical rainforest as big as about 20 football fields is cut or burnt down.

Why are the forests being cleared away? There are many reasons. All over the world, trees are cut down to make room for more houses, roads, and railway lines. In countries where there are many poor people with little land to live on, trees are cleared to grow vegetables or raise animals. In Central America, a quarter of the rainforest has been cleared for cattle-grazing land in the last 25 years. Almost all the beef raised on this land ends up as hamburgers in North American fast-food restaurants. In the northern United States and in Canada, many trees are cut down for lumber, and for pulp and paper. In fact, pulp and paper is Canada's biggest industry.

How many valuable things can you think of that come from trees? Let's see: there are apples, oranges, and lots of other fruits. There are walnuts, almonds, and coconuts. There are wooden chairs and tables and walls and floors — not to mention hockey sticks, skis, and tennis rackets. But the list doesn't stop there. Did you know that coffee, chocolate, and spices such as cinnamon, cloves, and nutmeg come from trees? Lots of medicines and chemicals are made from tree bark and leaves too.

Trees do other important things that we don't usually think about. Most of the animals in the world make their homes in forests. A forest is not just a stand of trees. It's a wonderful, busy community of insects, spiders, birds, and mammals of all kinds.

The great rainforests are called the "lungs of the world." They clean carbon dioxide out of the air, and put back oxygen and water. When big rainforests are cut down, there are changes in the soil and even in the weather. A lot of the water that rainforest trees give off falls again as rain. If the trees are gone, there is less rain. Some scientists think that cutting down the rainforests could change the climate of the whole world, making it hotter and drier.

Maybe the most important role trees have is to cling to the soil with their roots. Even when there are bad storms, trees can usually hold on. They break the wind and protect other plants and animals. In dry weather, tree roots hold the soil and keep it from blowing away with the wind. In wet weather, forests act like giant sponges. Tree roots hold the soil, which traps the rainwater. Then the water can run off slowly and evenly. If the trees are gone, though, the water can wash across the land too quickly, causing floods and carrying away soil. The wearing away of soil by wind and water is called *erosion*.

Have you ever walked down a road on a hot day and then cut into the woods? Right away you notice how much cooler it is among the trees. The canopy of leafy branches shades you from the sun. The air is moist and fresh on your skin. Sit down under a tree and wait quietly for a few minutes. You'll soon notice all the life that is humming, chirping, and scurrying around you, from millipedes to squirrels. You can see and feel for yourself that forests are some of the world's greatest treasures.

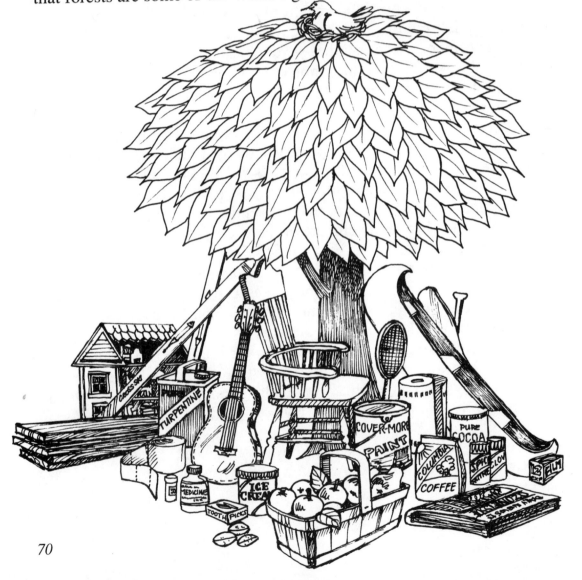

See Plants Breathe

Green plants are very important for animal life, because they produce oxygen that animals breathe. This is why the great rainforests are called "the lungs of the world." Here's a way to see the oxygen that plants "breathe out" through their leaves.

What You Need:
a large bowl
a wide-mouthed, clear glass jar
some water plants (pond weeds
    from a pond or water plants
    from a pet store that sells
    aquarium supplies)

What to Do:
1. Fill the bowl with water. Put the water plants in the bottom.

2. Lower the glass jar into the bowl sideways, so that it fills up with water. Then turn the jar upside down to cover the plants.

3. Put the bowl and jar in a sunny place. Leave it a few hours and then take a close look at the jar.

What's Happening?
You will soon see little streams of bubbles rising in the water in the jar. These are bubbles of oxygen coming from the water plants. In the same way — although you can't see it — land plants put oxygen into the air. If you leave the water plants under glass a little longer, you will see a pocket of air form at the top of the jar.

Gone with the Water

Do plant roots really stop erosion? Find out for yourself.

1. Grass to the Rescue?

What You Need:
2 metal pie plates
a watering can
potting soil
grass seed
2 buckets or other containers to
    catch runoff water
newspapers or a sheet of plastic
a measuring cup

What to Do:

1. Fill one of the pie plates with potting soil.

2. Sprinkle grass seed on the soil in the first pie plate. Press the seeds into the soil. Water this pie plate.

3. Put your first pie plate in a sunny spot and water it twice a day. In 2 to 3 weeks, you will have a little crop of sprouting grass.

4. Fill the second pie plate with potting soil.

5. Once you have a crop of grass in the first plate, set the two pie plates side by side on the edge of a table. Wedge something under them so that they slant a bit toward the table edge. (How much of a slant? Enough that water will trickle down the pie plates, but not so much that the soil will tip out!) Set both pie plates on the same slant.

6. If you are doing this activity inside, spread newspapers or a sheet of plastic on the floor to catch any spilled water. Indoors *or* outdoors, put a bucket or other container below each pie plate to catch water.

7. Measure out 1/2 cup (250 mL) of water, and pour it into the watering can. Gently pour water on the pie plate with just soil in it. Now gently pour the same amount of water on the pie plate with grass growing in it.

8. How much water trickles into the bucket under the plain soil plate? How much of the soil goes along with it? How much water trickles into the bucket under the plate with grass growing in it? Where do you think erosion would be worse — on a dirt-covered hillside or on a grass-covered hillside?

2. Plowing to Save Soil

What You Need:
2 cookie sheets
potting soil
2 buckets
a watering can

What to Do:
1. Fill the cookie sheets with soil.

2. Use your fingers to "plow" furrows in the soil. On one sheet, plow straight lines from the top to the bottom. On the other sheet, make one long snake-like furrow that goes back and forth across the sheet. (See the drawing.) This second pattern is called "contour plowing."

3. Follow the same steps you used in the first activity (Grass to the Rescue?). Place the sheets on a slant. Water them. Compare the amount of water and soil that runs off. Which plowing pattern do you think a farmer should use on a hillside?

AMAZING FACT

Medicines from the Rainforest

Did you know that about half the medicines doctors prescribe are made from plants? Plants that can cure diseases have been found all over the world, but tropical rainforests are the richest source of plant medicines. For instance, 70 percent of the plants that can help people who have cancer come from rainforests. This isn't really so surprising. Even though rainforests cover only about 10 percent of the Earth, about *half* the world's flowering plants are found in them.

Thousands of rainforest plants, however, have never been tested to see how they could help people. As the rainforests are cut down, many of these plants are disappearing. About 200 acres (80 hectares) of rainforest have been cut down since you started reading this page. Perhaps we human beings have lost wonderful medicines that we'll never know about.

New Paper from Newspaper

Recycle some paper and do your part to save trees.

What You Need:

water
8 pages of newspaper (or 4 double
    sheets)
extra newspapers
a plastic bucket
a medium-size saucepan
liquid dishwashing detergent
a colander
rubber gloves
an electric blender
a large mixing bowl
a stirring spoon
a square of fine wire mesh, about
    8 inches x 8 inches (20 cm x
    20 cm)
10 to 12 clean absorbent cloths
    ("absorbent" means they can
    soak up liquid) — old tea towels
    or cloth diapers would work
    well
a heavy book or other weight

What to Do:

1. Tear the newspaper into long, thin strips. Put the strips in the bucket and cover them with tap water. Leave them to soak overnight.

2. Next morning, pour off any water that has not soaked into the paper. Put the paper into the saucepan. Add 1 tablespoon (15 mL) of liquid detergent to the saucepan. Cover the paper with tap water again.

3. Put the saucepan on the stove, and heat it on low heat for 2 hours. Every once in awhile, check to make sure the paper is still covered with water. Add a little water if you need to.

4. Over the sink, *carefully* pour the mixture of water and paper mush from the saucepan into the colander. The water will pass through, and the paper mush will stay in the colander.

5. Run cold tap water over the paper mush in the colander. Stir the paper a bit to help the water strain through.

6. The next step uses the electric blender. *Don't use the blender without permission from a grownup.* Put on the rubber gloves. Take a handful of soggy paper and put it into the blender. Add tap water until the blender container is 3/4 full. Switch the blender on for a few seconds and then switch it off. Continue this switching for about 1 minute.

7. Pour the blended mush — called pulp — into a large plastic mixing bowl.

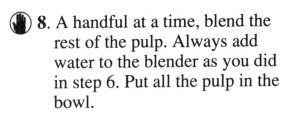

8. A handful at a time, blend the rest of the pulp. Always add water to the blender as you did in step 6. Put all the pulp in the bowl.

9. Add water to the bowl of pulp until it is half full. Use a large stirring spoon to stir the water into the pulp.

10. Lay an absorbent piece of cloth on a flat surface. (If you are using a table that can be damaged by water, put a sheet of plastic under the cloth.)

11. Slide the wire mesh into the bowl. You want to get a thin, even coating of pulp on the mesh. If the first dipping doesn't work well, try this step again.

12. This is a tricky step. Bring the coated wire mesh to the cloth. Quickly and smoothly lay the mesh on the cloth, pulp side down.

13. Press the mesh hard against the cloth. Now lift the mesh, leaving the pulp behind on the cloth. Put another piece of cloth over the pulp. Press hard again.

14. Repeat steps 12 and 13 on top of the first cloth pulp "sandwich." Keep doing this until you run out of pulp. End with a cloth. Now you have many layers of cloth and pulp. Put a heavy weight on top of the stack to keep it pressed down. (You might want to put a sheet of plastic on top of your stack to keep your paper presser from getting wet.) Leave the stack — with its paper presser on top — for 24 hours.

15. Carefully peel off the pieces of damp paper and put them on newspaper to dry. Now you can make your own recycled greeting cards or decorated notepaper. And you can print on the back: Recycled by *(your name)* to save a tree.

Weird Trees

The elephant tree of northern Mexico wants to hold onto the few leaves it has. If any creature tugs at its leaves, the tree gives out a horrible, stinky mist that covers everything within 3 feet (1 m). Leaf-eaters quickly learn to nibble on something else!

The rare welwitschia tree of Africa has a trunk about 3 feet (1 m) in diameter. (The diameter is the distance from one side of the trunk to the other.) However, the whole tree is only about 12 inches (30 cm) high. Stranger still, the welwitschia only has *two* leaves. These leaves grow very long, and get so battered by wind and sand that they look like a lot of ragged crepe paper streamers.

The banyan tree of India seems to have everything backwards. It sprouts roots from its *branches*. These roots then have to work their way down to the ground. When they finally root themselves in the earth, they become as thick and woody as extra tree trunks. Some large banyans have as many as 350 root "trunks." One tree ends up looking like a small forest!

Taking Care of Our Home

*I*f someone asked you where you lived, what would you say? You'd probably give your street address, or the name of your city or town. But can you see now that the larger environment you share with other animals and plants is also your home? We don't spread garbage around inside our houses, and we shouldn't do it in nature, either. We need clean air, pure water, soil, and sunlight to keep us alive and healthy.

For most of the time that human beings have lived on Earth, there weren't many of us. Our tools were simple. Nature seemed vast. We could pull up plants and kill animals for our use, and the supply never ran out. The Earth could recycle our wastes. We could just take what we needed from nature and feel pretty sure there would always be more. Why can't we live that way now?

One reason is that human beings have been able to invent so many useful things, such as medicines and tractors and refrigerators. All these inventions have helped us eat better, stay healthier, and live longer. It was only about 1830 that the human population reached 1 billion. Now, about 160 years later, there are 5 billion people. In your lifetime, the Earth's population will probably double again to 10 billion! And remember that each new person has to have a place to live, food, clothing, air to breathe, and water to drink.

There are huge numbers of human beings now. But that's not the only problem. Modern people have invented machines such as chainsaws that let us cut down trees with frightening speed. We have bulldozers that level land

and fill in ponds and marshes. We have huge factories that spew poisons into the air and water. We spread deadly chemicals on farmland. These chemicals end up in our food and water. Our cars pollute the air. We are ruining the habitats of other animals, and poisoning the air, water, and soil that all living things need.

Many of us know that we have to break our old habits of pouring things into rivers, dumping wastes onto the ground, and letting gas and smoke escape into the air. We have the skills and knowledge to clean up our home, the Earth. All we need is the *desire* to do it.

And that's where kids come in. *You* will inherit what your parents and other grownups leave of the world. Often adults work so hard to get ahead in life that they don't stop to think about the long-term effects of what they're doing. Where will the animals go when forests are cut down? Where will we get our drinking water — and where will we swim — if we put sewage and chemicals in our lakes, rivers, and seas? Many adults forget to ask these questions. You can keep reminding them that your future is being affected by what they are doing today.

And you don't have to wait until you're grown up to help the environment yourself. Look at the list of 28 things you can do to save the environment, on p.86. Perhaps you can think of other ways, too. Urge your family to follow your example and spread the word to your friends. It may seem to you that you're not doing very much, but if all kids worked at looking after the environment, it would add up to a lot.

The Native peoples of North America can teach us about respecting the Earth. They look on whales, ravens, and other living creatures as their brothers and sisters. The Native people think of land and trees and water as things to take care of. Isn't it time the rest of us started thinking that way, too?

Energy Savers

In cold parts of the country, people try to conserve energy by insulating their homes and putting weatherstripping around doors and windows. Do these things really make a difference?

What You Need:
water
a glass
a cardboard carton that closes, big enough to hold the glass
a thermometer
some cotton balls or sheets of crumpled newspaper
some heavy tape
scissors
a refrigerator
a pencil and paper

What to Do:
1. Put the glass, filled with room-temperature water, into the box. Poke a hole in the lid of the box and stick the thermometer through. Put the thermometer into the glass of water.

2. Put the box into the refrigerator. Every 3 minutes, read the thermometer and write down the reading. Do this until the temperature falls to 4°C (40° F). How long did this take?

3. Start again with a glass of water at room temperature. This time, pack cotton balls or crumpled newspaper all around the glass. Put the box back into the refrigerator and take temperature readings again. Is the temperature falling faster now, or more slowly? Do you think the insulation around the glass is working?

4. Cut slots in the sides of the cardboard box. Once again, put a glass full of room-temperature water into the box. Put the box into the refrigerator. Take temperature readings the way

you did before. Write them down. Is the temperature falling more quickly or more slowly than it did without the slots? Why?

5. Start again with a new glass of room-temperature water. This time, tape over the slots in the box with heavy tape. Take temperature readings again. The tape works like weather-stripping. Does it help keep cold air out of the box?

AMAZING FACT

Deadly Ghost Nets

Many modern fishing fleets catch fish in gill nets. These tough nets are made of fibers that never rot. They can trail 25 miles (40 km) out into the ocean. Gill nets don't catch fish in a pouch. Instead, they simply tangle fish by their gills. These invisible nets also snare anything else that hits them. Millions of sea birds and mammals have been killed this way. A study of North Pacific gill nets set for salmon found that they killed many other sea creatures too: 750,000 sea birds, 20,000 porpoises, 700 fur seals, and many small whales. Remember, this was in just one part of the Pacific in just one year. Worse, ships sometimes throw away unwanted gill nets into the sea. These can trail for years as "ghost nets." They keep on catching fish that will never be hauled in, and killing everything else in their path, too.

Helping Hands and Flippers

The people of Tokerau Beach, New Zealand, woke up one morning to find 80 pilot whales stranded in shallow surf. Everybody waded into the water to help. The people knew how to aid the whales without upsetting or injuring them. They didn't try to push the whales out to sea while the tide was low. Instead, they stayed in the water with the whales, keeping their skin wet until the tide turned. They talked to the whales in soft, soothing voices. When the tide came in, they struggled to turn the whales around and haul them into deeper water.

At this point, something amazing happened. A school of dolphins swam in toward shore and mingled with the whales. Soon the dolphins were leading the whales out to sea. This might sound farfetched, but it has happened before in New Zealand. A helicopter pilot once watched dolphins guide beached whales several kilometres out into the ocean. Dolphins are coastal animals. They know the bays and inlets better than the deep-sea whales do. And it seems that the dolphins are willing to share what they know with bewildered visitors.

Make Your Own Solar Panel

Most of our homes are heated by *nonrenewable* resources — oil and natural gas. "Nonrenewable" means that once they're taken from the ground, we can't make more. But the Sun is a source of energy that isn't going to run out for billions of years. Some people heat their water with solar panels on their roofs. You can find out for yourself how a solar panel works.

What You Need:
2 plastic dishpans, the same size
a black plastic garbage bag
heavy tape or twine
a big bucket of water, or a hose
2 thermometers
paper and a pencil
a pane of glass or clear plastic, big
    enough to cover a dishpan
a bright, sunny day

What to Do:
1. At about 10 a.m., put your 2 dishpans outside in a sunny place. Put the black garbage bag inside one dishpan, so that it covers the bottom and sides. Use heavy tape or twine to hold it firmly in place.

2. Fill the dishpans with cold water. If you have to carry the

water in a bucket, you may need an adult to help you.

3. Use the thermometer to measure the air temperature. Then measure the temperature of the water in the dishpans. Write these down.

4. Lay the pane of glass or plastic on the dishpan with the garbage bag in it. If you're using a glass pane, have an adult help you.

The dishpan with the pane and garbage bag is your solar panel.

5. Once an hour, for the next 4 hours, measure the air temperature. Then measure the temperature in each dishpan. What do you find? What's the point of having a second dishpan, *not* made into a solar panel? Could you find out just as much about how a solar panel works with just one dishpan?

What's Happening?

When a solar panel is used to heat water for a house, it works like this. The solar panel is a large, shallow box sitting on the roof. The bottom of the box is metal, painted black. Black absorbs (soaks up) the Sun's rays better than other colors. The box is covered with glass. Pipes run through the box, between the metal and the glass. Water flows through the pipes. As the sun shines on the box, it heats up inside. The water flowing through the pipes heats up, too. It continues on through more pipes into the house. Then someone can take a nice, hot shower .

28 Things You — and Your Family — Can Do Right Now to Save the Environment

There are many easy things that you and your family can do every day to put less strain on the environment.

1. Before throwing letter-size paper into the garbage, check the backs of sheets to see if they're blank. If so, use them for drawing. Or cut them into squares and use them as notepaper beside the phone.

2. Reuse big envelopes that arrive in the mail. Just put a new address label on — any square of paper will do — and send them out again.

3. Most families get many pieces of junk mail. These are a great waste of paper if you don't want them and don't read them. Send pieces of junk mail back where they came from — at the mailers' expense. Tell the mailers you don't want any more.

4. If possible, take showers instead of baths. Showers use less water than baths. Soap up and *then* turn the shower head on.

5. Don't throw out those last little bits of soap. Stick them to the next bar.

6. Don't use the toilet as a garbage can. For instance, don't throw a facial tissue into the toilet after blowing your nose. Throw it into a wastebasket instead.

7. Don't pour anything from a container marked "poisonous" or "dangerous" into the sink or onto the ground.

8. Buy pump spray containers, which work just as well as aerosol cans, and don't harm the atmosphere.

9. Compost your kitchen leftovers, such as apple cores and potato peelings. You'll be amazed at how much less garbage you have. And your garden will be grateful.

10. Buy eggs in cardboard cartons, not styrofoam ones.

11. For foods that don't spoil quickly, buy the biggest size you can afford. First, the biggest size is usually the best buy. Second, there's less packaging for the amount of stuff you get. For instance, a big box of cereal is cheaper and has less wrapping than a carton of one-serving boxes.

14. Find out if your community has depots (or even curbside pickups) to recycle bottles, cans, and paper. Then make sure that you and your family recycle these things. If your community has no recycling program, read on:

12. Buy some foods, such as raisins and dried beans, in bulk. Even supermarkets have bulk bins now. You can reuse your own containers. Besides, bulk buying is usually cheaper than buying packaged products.

13. Write letters complaining to companies that use lots of wasteful, polluting packaging on their products. (This includes many toy companies and fast-food restaurants.) Support companies that try to put their products in simple packages that can be recycled.

15. Write to the mayor of your town or city and urge him or her to begin a recycling program for waste paper, glass, and metal.

16. Ask your teachers to see whether your school can be a recycling depot for paper, glass, and metal. Often a class can raise money for school projects by recycling.

17. You'll probably *have* to buy some things in plastic containers, because that's the only way they're sold. If they go into the garbage, they'll be polluting the environment for a long, long time. What else can you do with them? You can use big ice-cream containers as flour canisters or crayon containers. Ice-cream and margarine containers can be fridge keepers or plant pots. Little yogurt cups make great paint containers. If you can't use them, nursery schools and day-care centers usually want them. There are craft books at the library that tell you how to make gifts out of old containers. Find out how crafty you can be.

18. Become a saver. Giftwrap paper can be smoothed out and used again. So can ribbon and string. Make gift tags from the fronts of old greeting cards.

19. Use rags — worn-out clothes, sheets, and (softest of all) old cloth diapers — for housecleaning instead of paper towels and throwaway cleaning cloths.

20. Don't throw away outgrown or unwanted clothes. Maybe there is someone else in your family or neighborhood that the clothes could be passed on to. You can also sell the clothes to a second-hand store, or give them to a charity that will pass them on to needy people.

21. Don't throw litter (gum wrappers, plastic bags, soft-drink cans, and so on) onto the ground or into creeks and ponds.

22. Turn the thermostat down and wear a sweater. Turn the thermostat down even more at night, when everybody's cosy under their blankets anyway.

23. Turn off: the TV when nobody's watching it; the lights when you leave a room.

24. If you can, walk or ride your bike instead of asking for a car ride. It's better for you, saves energy, and cuts down on pollution.

25. When you use an electric appliance, make sure you get all you can out of the electricity you're using. For instance, try to dry a few things in the clothes dryer at once. Don't turn it on for just one blouse or a pair of socks.

26. When you have a choice, buy the product that runs on human energy instead of a battery or electricity. For instance, do you really need an electric toothbrush? Your dentist can show you how to do a great job of brushing your teeth with an ordinary toothbrush.

27. Talk to your parents, other relatives, and friends about the environment and how we can protect it. Share ideas for saving energy and recycling things.

28. Your family probably makes some donations to charities and other groups every year. Is your family supporting a group that works to clean up the environment?

Index